Thoughtful Gifts

A Division of The McGraw·Hill Companies

Columbus, Ohio

www.sra4kids.com

SRA/McGraw-Hill

A Division of The **McGraw·Hill** *Companies*

Send all inquiries to:
SRA/McGraw-Hill
8787 Orion Place
Columbus, OH 43240-4027

ISBN 0-07-569837-4
   3 4 5 6 7 8 9 DBH 05 04 03 02

Kate, Mike, and Sue wanted to get thoughtful gifts for Joe on his birthday.

Kate bought a book about dinosaurs. The dinosaurs in the book fought a lot!

Mike bought a set of markers. He thought the markers looked like a rainbow.

Sue bought a kite. She thought the kite looked like a dragon in the sky.

The children brought the gifts to Joe's birthday party. Joe's mom brought out the birthday cake.

Joe liked his terrific gifts.
He thanked his thoughtful pals.